Firefighters

Written by Barrie Wade
Photographed by Paul Moore
Illustrated by Pauline Rosenthal

Collins *Educational*
An imprint of HarperCollins*Publishers*

 The fire engines are at the fire station.
They are ready to set off.

 The firefighters are ready, too.

 The firefighters set off, in the fire engine.

 Sometimes they go to a road accident.

Sometimes they go to fight a fire.

 Fire hoses bring water

to fight the fire.

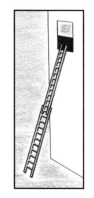

Firefighters climb
long ladders

to fight fires in
high buildings.

 Firefighters fight fires in smoke.

So they
sometimes
have to put
on masks.

 Firefighters are always ready.

 But fire is dangerous.

 So don't play with fire!